To Nia-
Always let
your inner sparkle
shine!

The Little Unicorn

Written by Sheri Fink

Illustrations by Lynx Animation Studios

Books by Sheri Fink:

The Little Rose
The Little Gnome
The Little Firefly
Exploring the Garden with the Little Rose
The Little Seahorse
Counting Sea Life with the Little Seahorse

THE LITTLE UNICORN
By Sheri Fink

Text and illustrations copyright © 2018 by Sheri Fink

The Little Unicorn character is inspired by the work of Mary Erikson Washam.

Library of Congress Control Number: 2018906087
ISBN: 978-1-949213-00-3

Printed in China
FIRST EDITION

This book is dedicated with love and gratitude to my amazing husband, Derek Taylor Kent, who made me believe in magic beyond my wildest dreams.

Deep within an enchanted forest lived a magical Little Unicorn. The forest was a happy place filled with beautiful plants, sweet-smelling flowers, and friendly animals. The friendliest of all was the Little Unicorn.

She loved sharing joy with the world around her. She whispered wishes to the trees, blew kisses to the butterflies, and sang songs to the flower fairies every day.

One of her favorite things to do was visit the shimmering pond at the end of the rainbow river. She would gaze at her reflection in the water, thinking happy thoughts.

When she thought of things that made her feel grateful, her emerald green eyes would sparkle and a new fairy would be born.

As she grew, the Little Unicorn sometimes wondered about the places she was told not to explore.

One day, when curiosity got the best of her, she ventured into an unknown part of the forest that was gloomier than the lush, colorful home she knew and loved.

There were trees that looked as if moss had grown on them for hundreds of years. Menacing eyes glowed all around her, and there was a wet, sticky feeling in the air.

A brisk breeze ruffled the Little Unicorn's rainbow mane and gave her a chill. For a moment, she wondered if she would be able to find her way home.

But, the Little Unicorn was brave and continued onward. She hoped that her magic might be able to brighten this dreary place, but it didn't seem to work.

She had been wandering for hours and needed a refreshing drink of water. Hearing a chorus of frogs croaking nearby, she approached a murky pond.

When she peered into the pond in this unfamiliar place, she couldn't think of anything to feel grateful for, nor could she see her sparkle. This had never happened to her.

She had a frightening thought—**what if she had lost her sparkle forever?**

Shocked and scared, she tried again and again, but it never appeared.

As night fell, she still hadn't found her way home. The Little Unicorn spotted a cozy cave and decided to take refuge there. When she awakened the next morning, she hoped that it was all a bad dream.

She returned to the murky pond again and gazed at her muddled reflection. Still, to her dismay, there was no sparkle reflecting in the water. Even worse, she noticed that she was starting to lose the color from her rainbow mane!

The Little Unicorn felt completely lost. Her sparkle was what she believed made her special.

Who would she be without it?

She wandered and wandered until she finally found her way back to the enchanted forest. When she arrived, she barely recognized it as her magical home. It was cold and grey. All of the lollipop flowers had lost their color. The Little Unicorn hung her head in sadness.

Just then, a little fairy flitted over to her. "Thank gumdrops you've returned! The forest has lost its magic and all my friends have fluttered away."

"It's my fault," replied the Little Unicorn, holding back her tears. "I've lost my sparkle."

"Wickety spickets!" said the little fairy.
"Then we just have to go find it!"

So the Little Unicorn embarked on a mission with the little fairy to find her sparkle. They searched high and low and far and wide looking in every pool, river, and waterfall, but her precious sparkle was nowhere to be found.

When they returned to their once sunny, but now dismal home, the Little Unicorn began to cry. She didn't know what to do and felt embarrassed that her colors were nearly gone.

The little fairy tried to console her. **"Don't worry,"** she said, **"we'll always have each other, and friendship is its own kind of magic."**

Realizing that she had found a true friend, the Little Unicorn shed tears of joy that rolled down her cheeks and formed a puddle around her. Despite her sadness, she felt grateful to have the little fairy by her side.

As the Little Unicorn looked into the puddle, she felt love bubble up inside, and suddenly, her sparkle reflected back to her! She thought of the buttercups and bees in the meadow, the sweet smell of orange blossoms on the wind, and the happy songs of birds chirping in the treetops.

At that moment, she realized that it was never the sunshine, the colors, or the lollipop flowers that made the forest magical. It was her loving presence.

Her vibrant rainbow colors returned to her mane and tail. She trotted around touching each plant and animal with her horn, reigniting their radiance.

Dozens of baby fairies burst forth from the flowers and joined in the celebration!

The Little Unicorn understood that, like the sun hiding behind a curtain of clouds, her sparkle was always inside of her longing to shine its magic.

Only when she doubted herself did her sparkle dim. She continued spreading love and kindness, and her sparkle glowed more brilliantly year after year.

She and her forest friends lived happily
(and sparkly) ever after.

Just like the Little Unicorn, you can create magic when you believe in yourself and cherish your friends. Your sparkle is always within you and shines brightest when you spread love, joy, and kindness. Never let anything dim your sparkle.